URBAN SCRIBE
<u>THE CITIES HEART BEAT</u>

BY FIRST TIME POET:

ANTHONY L. ANDERSON

ISBN: 0-7596-8201-1

This book is printed on acid free paper.

1stBooks - rev. 3/8/02

This Collection Of Poems Is Dedicated To
(Big Jim & Ollie Mae)

and

My Light and Inspiration
(Tina)

<u>ADDRESSES UNKNOWN</u>

Beyond heavens gates
pass the visible stars
my place exist.

My neighbors
v.i.p.'s all consisted
of love, devotion, and
faith.

Quiet my neighborhood is
until stirred by emotion
a deep yearning to seal
what lie's beyond.

IN SEARCH OF

The ability to grasp,
my option to choose,
to hold in awe
praying to never lose.

In search of for years,
the heartache that came
to have found my place,
once spoken your name.

HER BIRTH

The combinations were endless
blind chances
worth taking.

The anticipated results
of a love that was in the making,
joy of the new
many years to watch grow

Infant to adult
and the unseen world
she'll know.

<u>LOVES OTHER MEANING</u>

Within the spoken word
lie's a secret darkness
not the beginning
nor the end.

A place where light
is unwanted
a darkness lit
with meaning.

A passion unseen
contemplate the unspoken
your peaceful search
revived.

<u>THE UNNECESSARY ("SORRY")</u>

The brazenness, the complete gall
to attempt to form the
sentence.

Callously you stole
a life force not created
by you

Your actions uncivilized
reasons non-existent
damnation your reward
pity none given.

GIVE AND TAKE

What exist within one
to share unselfishly,
express what's truly
real,

Willing to give
indefinitely.

Extend beyond your limits
to soar where only God
knows,

Ability to understand
truly a lovers goal.

<u>MONDAY</u>

Hell if I know
maybe I'm not
suppose to.

Yet my movement
continues on.

Need not complain

Silence seems to
be my key.

ANDERSON V. COMMONWEALTH

<u>"RAGE AGAINST THE STATE"</u>

They said it was over
could nothing really be done
forfeited my future
property of a savage one.

Justified within their thinking
answered only to the machine,

Feelings

Your kidding unacceptable
blinded by sheer greed.

Rehab never played a part
bottom line is all that matters,
pray and self discipline to guide
you through.

Fuck it,
judgement day
it will do…

<u>SPEAK FOR YOURSELF</u>

Traveling within my
inner thoughts,
in search of
tranquility.

Prioritize the best I can,

Backwards world I live in.

To move about through faceless
forms, exist within
myself,

Complete separation from
all the norm,

Rational contemplation put on
the shelf.

"TO BE CONTINUED"

MANHOOD UNGUARDED

His essence he gave fervently
the gift to her to explore
his most guarded virtue.

Years it took to develop,
patiently building the wall
that hid away his most
prized possession.

But to her he freely gave
in, to the beauty that
illuminated from her
melted away the machismo.

The façade that masquerades
his weakness, and at the
end of intense passion, her
Meaning unveiled, pure
lust, no attachments.

<u>ALL PRAISES DO...</u>

Eye's to the east
five times a day,
a true joy from
observing,

Extend your knowledge to
the common man,
in his kingdom your's
most deserving.

His greatness for all
to know,
his forgiveness everlasting.

Fall and give praise
on your knee's
his eye's constantly
watching.

WHO THE HELL CARES

As loud as I speak
as hard as I try,
my words fall on
deaf ears.

Within lie's a secret
to change many lives
but no-one seems to
care.

But again I press on
with no real success
failure not my friend,

Until I reach my
elusive dreams, I'll
scream till heaven
Opens…

<u>MY SONG FOR TINA...</u>

The years will intertwine
seasons constantly change
a true love from a
sincere romantic.

God's secret gift was
shared with us,
no options to take
for granted.

The words I speak
all feelings I share
for you and you alone,

For I have found
what has taken me
years,

We shall carve our
bond in stone.

ANTHONY L. ANDERSON

STILL CAN HEAR YOU

A TRIBUTE TO MILES, DIZZY, AND THE MONK.

PLAY GROVER

Inside this dimly lit room,
made even more obscure from
the stale cigar smoke, I
heard them.

Vocalization an unnecessary
purpose, in tune with each
lyric.

From each note, I swear
I heard them all, the
great one's who've gone
before us.

The vibe kind of haunting,
but not afraid to let it in.

For some strange reason
it seems to speak
directly to me.

Their notes overwhelming
and invading my
process.

IT'S COOL THOUGH,
JAZZ SHOULD BE THIS
WAY…

<u>MY FATHERS PRAYER'S</u>
<u>BIG JIM'S THE NAME...</u>

Quietly he goes through
life, complaining not his
style.

For all his years the light
still bright knowing his
God walks by his side.

To stroll in his footsteps
an honor unmatched,
absorb his knowledge
if you can.

For the strength he's
shown unconditional love,
what could only fit.

AMEN...

<u>BUSTED</u>

The repetitions became
almost numbing, I slowly
searched each word for the
hidden meaning.

Never was one for riddles
my world not seen through
rose colored glasses.

But yet, still can't find
her, somewhere within these
ten pages of pain her meaning
still escapes me.

But because of (LOVE)
I start from the beginning,
oh damn it's becoming clear
to me now.

No longer is this a riddle,
the now noticeable stain on
each page of her letter.

Removed my ego from this
picture, my sad moment of
clarity had finally arrived.

I knew that lady in the
hotel lobby looked familiar
college buddies from back
east.

One phone call from her
was all it took.

And because of lust,

MY WHOLE WORLD IS GONE…

PEDEE-MAE...

Within her eye's, the gentle
touch all healings do flow so
easily.

The pain she endured to bring
you here, lord knows she'd do
again freely.

To express to her what she means
to you words just refuse to flow,
but you search your thoughts and
rack your brain cause joyfully
you just have to let her know.

They set aside just one free day
for siblings to pay their blessings,

But all year round your love is
felt one day is just not addressing.

I take this time to share with you,
what I think you already know
your love, support and constant care,
makes my entire world glow.

THE REAL LIBERTY.

Gone all that I know
replaced with just misery,
my shells existence is day to day
but for what, is there an end
unseen?

Has my curtain call been
announced, hell I don't
know can't hear it or
just choose to ignore it.

But I trek on not to
wade in self-pity
definitely not built
that way.

Because behind that door,
just on the other side of
despair lie's my salvation.

Weak men don't finish no need
to enter the race.

Hold your head up black man,
numbered are their days…

<u>AT YOUR OWN RISK.</u>

Lights turned out
have closed my eye's
to dream a world unknown.

Searched inside for
peace of mind, a nightmare
soon to unfold.

Forced myself to awaken,
I can't have gone too deep.

To dream my dreams inside
this world, will soon be
the death of me…

A MASTER PIECE...

I wish to paint you
in abstract form, a new
vision is what I crave.

To mold you in obscure
lines, to define your
seductive ways.

In search of your
true meaning a life's
work worth
undertaking.

To expose your beauty for
the world, a blessing not
man made...

CRACKER, DON'T LOOK NOW

<u>WE'RE HEEEEEEERRRRRE...</u>

The mission to make
you defer again a major
task their undertaking.

Break your spirit, shame
to your name with nerve to
smile in your face.

Send them back they all
cry, scared of what the
Future will bring.

Many years of bondage, en
slaved to the man, a
Revolutions cry soon to
ring...

<u>WINDS OF CHANGE</u>

Through my window as
gentle as can be the
night breezes cool my skin.

The many seasons that have
come and gone enough to make
My heart bleed.

Calming, thoughts of days
gone by, erupt memory's
from deep within.

For as long as I feel the
winds of change truly comforts
all my sufferings.

VIOLENT IMAGES...

Find a way to channel it
or place it on the shelf, for
the emotion your choosing to let
out surely will destroy
yourself.

Look at the examples before you,
their screaming for you to hear.

What is it are you
searching for can only
end in despair.

Anger just takes to much
energy a commodity you
should reserve.

Just too much you can lose
from an action considered
absurd...

<u>EXPRESSIONS IN BLACK AND WHITE...</u>

The words I used to describe
you run abundantly through my
mind.

But lost as I am inside your
gaze, so hard to form a proper
rhyme.

That's why as I write each loving word
to express just how I feel,
To know what God has shared with me,
a love for a life time to show
all others,
it does exist and is definitely real.

Inside my dreams you have found
your place, removed what you thought
was best.

Nightmares of the past no longer
exist, replaced with your tenderness...

YEAH I SAID IT...

What monuments, what apology has really
ever been given.

Reparation to damn late KEEP IT pity's
unacceptable in my humble opinion.

You've built walls for soldiers who
gave their lives in far and distant
lands, they fought your battles won
your damn wars, but back home treated
dead wrong, completely dis-respected
for what?
(OH YEAH) bein a black man.

Affirmative action many do cry, another form
of government assistance, to depend on them
to even the score (YOUR KIDDING) their
keeping you in these conditions.

They say things have gotten better for who,
the one or two percent, to go by those numbers
to be that damn blind, your conditions you
continue to suffer in.

BACK OFF...

You would be amazed
at the many who pass blind
judgement on those they feel
inferior.

Could it be ignorance,
or maybe just fear.

remember a mirror has
two sides to it.

And your reflection
cast many different
aspersions, to the masses...

<u>WRONG ANSWER...</u>

Gone are the day's
of talking things out,
a gun now the child's
voice, who's to blame?

<u>NOT ME...</u>

No such thing as
being alone, thoughts
do keep good
company...

CLOCK'S TICKING...

Time to strike back
and hope you do mind,
can't except no more from
you.

We shall overcome straight
Bullshit, no more singing
We're through.

You only seem to respect
violence, though peace we've
tried for years.

Time to wake up
your battle draws close,
oh guess what no fear....

HEAR ME!!
"YA TRICK"...

MY BROTHER LISTEN

<u>JUST SAY NO...</u>

Black man do you hear me, or
have you gone to far to
comprehend I'm reaching out
to you.

Been gone a long time didn't
think you were coming back, but
glad to see you, and you look
strong too.

Guess Mother Afrika was
right, told them all your
spirit to strong to stamp
out.

Now don't swell your ego
your journey far from
over, but it would appear
Your winning.

The struggle continues.

THE "N" WORD, HOPE YOUR HAPPY.

It flows from your lips so
comfortably, your completely
at peace with it's meaning.

How the hell did you get
so far off track, when did
you sell-out your dignity.

A label given to you by
butchers who raped and
burned your homeland.

It's meaning quite simply
not a term of endearment it
describes an endangered
species.

THE BLACK MAN...

<u>UNAMERICAN DREAM.</u>

Relocated, uprooted anyway
you put it, packed up your
ass was gone, shackled and
strapped in a pit of darkness
next stop, your new foreign
home.

<u>BYE-BYE</u>

How do I tell her I can't
lie, respect she truly deserves,
but this secret I hold inside
can't live like this don't possess
that nerve.

Days of a player far behind
me in search of my soul mate,
thought it was you god knows
I did, but this not love or
hate.

Can now describe what you
mean to me trying to justify
this end.

Once scar's have healed and
clarity's about you, please
think of me,

"YOUR FRIEND"

<u>MISS YOU...</u>

I can feel you,
your essence engulfs me.

Sweet breath upon my chest
a deep tingling with desire.

Your touch is comforting,
Complete peace with this
Sensual sensation.

Eye's of an angelic queen
completely hold me in a
Trance like state.

IF ONLY YOU WERE HERE...

THANK YOU...

Because of you it's
Existence within me
Has been awaken.

Once again the yearnings
locked away have been
touched by your light.

Inside this darkness
devoid of passion, fire
has again ignited my
nature.

Guarded armor of the
pass now locked away
replaced with trust,

Freely I give to you,
in return devotions reward...

<u>REACHING OUT.</u>

I've known loneliness,
it's a cold and bitter
thing.

I've experienced emptiness
hearts content never to
sing.

But love I have touched,
it's feel complete and
Engulfing.

Your essence, inner beauty
and all that surrounds you,

TRULY A HEAVENLY BLESSING...

DECEIT.

It's form takes on
many shapes, though it's
meaning is quite clear.

To string about, to play
the fake, to hell with
Others emotional fears.

Once your done you toss
aside oblivious to the pain
you've caused.

Turn about truly fair play,
in the end only your loss.

<u>DREAMS BUILT FOR TWO.</u>

My goals are lofty,
a task for one there
not.

The ambition that is
Within me something I
can't express alone.

Meaning to share part of
the plan selfish way's
Can't do.

Love in search of is the goal I
reach for, her touch the remedy
I pursue.

I DO...

As I stare into the
stars that are your eye's
the promise I bring can't
be attainable through words
to attempt clearly an under-
statement.

It is not written in any text
nor has it's secret been unveiled
to mere man.

For man's capability to grasp
the meaning of my true expression
to you falls an entire galaxy
to short.

As I stand before you my gift
to you is shared with only
one, for she is the only one
who could breathe into me the
Commitment in which I speak.

<u>CONTEMPLATIONS.</u>

Countless thought many
combinations an over abundance
of energy.

To encounter one so entrancing,
the enticement of her touch
un-mentionable.

Again how can I express within
human parameters the profound
depths in which her completeness
has altered my life's
rhythm.

A task now acknowledged as
impossible, the remedy.

To continually experience the
evolution of her glow.

SUNSHINE

Clouds of darkness which does
appear daily over me, it's stride
step for step in rhythm of my
hearts lonely beat.

It's heavy thunderous existence
is crashing inside my ears, to
all the world it's exposing my
raw and naked fears.

Strength of pride my only shield
from this beast which torments
me, my battle to fight my will
to win refuse to admit defeat.

Peer through these clouds, expose
the light, the warm sun of my
inner soul, cloud of darkness
despair within you will never
make me fold.

A CONTRAST IN DOING TIME.

How do I accomplish this,
where do I begin to justify
the pain I must place at
her doorstep.

The good the bad we dealt
with, somehow we made it
through, what's different now
are we not still the same people?

In love once, a place we owned
a piece of bliss that was ours
it's gone now replaced with vacancy
the question of what if, if only.

Time not our friend just the
opposite a mortal enemy did to us
what no-one else could do.

Destroyed our bond, disband our
love, drove a wedge through our
heart, ended our world, broken
and shattered in two.

REALITY CHECK

This environment looks familiar, I know I've been here many times before, oh yeah now I recognize this place and it's something to behold. To relive the many experiences that make up my life.

But there's a problem I can see it all, I can even relive them over and over but why can't I change the negative? If it's possible to see and even feel the past then why my father are you punishing me by not letting me fix the mistakes that make up a part of who I am.

<u>WOUNDS OF THE SOUL</u>

Why did this happen
all plans in place to supply
her every need.

Purest of intentions, this
feeling of bliss, what did I
do? How could she deceive.

My world to her was for the
taking, anything as long as
to please.

Exposed a tender side,
this man dropped his pride
Completely down on bended
knee's.

Life's teaching so hard the
Pain that comes within
time I'll understand.

To heal my wounds move
on with my life, this
experience made a stronger
man...

<u>PAIN</u>

It's existence is real
but it has no need to
speak.

The feeling so unbearable,
but to experience it alters
the very life's blood within
you.

It's form and shape has
many angles,
but it's recognizable to
all who look closely.

But to see it just look to
the eye's, souls window,
your view unforgettable.

KIM. PERROT

I watched you, the way
you enjoyed life the
fullest and all out.

I wish I knew you to
be able to bask in the
glow of maybe just your
friendship.

But who am I? Oh, just a
fan one of many admirer's to
have had the chance to see
you do what you enjoyed.

But I lived you, at least
a small portion through those
Who were always in your
presence.

And the shine within their
eye's said it all, you were
Real and your entire essence
truly a blessing.

I Miss You...

Sincerely (A FAN)...

<u>HER SECRET GIFT</u>

Please forgive me, for
the smile upon my face
exist for selfish reasons.

For a brief moment I
was allowed to peer into
your heart and exposed
something, your
vulnerability.

Along side your heart your
soul called out clearly and I
heard it, my name rolled from
it's core.

For me to see what you tried to
protect I again ask your forgiveness.

My intentions not to appear cocky,
nor stroke my ego with praise, but
with tenderness, protect and
nourish what I know you give.

THANK YOU...

<u>CONFIDENT.</u>

Your not paying attention
I don't think you even hear
the rejection I feel that
comes from you.

Attempt to share my joy,
helping fill your lonely void
your emotions run cold tell
me what's the use.

Raised me from a child empty
world for quite a while things
you said and did I forgave you.

But to treat me such as you do
the best thing for me and you
to distance ourselves in time and space
we're through.

<u>CONTRADICTIONS</u>

Time heals all wounds a
cliche for the ages.
spoken from someone who's
never truly experienced a loss.

I'm cold but yet the sun
shines ever so brightly upon me.

My thirst seems unquenchable
although before me spring waters
run deep, but not full am I.

Your hand lays upon my skin
soft as it could be, but truly
I feel no warmth coming from your
touch.

Eternity of time has passed,
my wound still fresh,
explain yourself?

New Cliche:

Ignorance must be your only
rule.

<u>WHERE ARE YOU...</u>

I see your tears and know the reason you cry them, and from deep within the core of my soul a hole widens.

Your voice I listen to and again what your expressing profoundly changes my perception on love.

The absence of your touch exposes the very fiber of my feelings for you.

To miss someone this much, a phenomenon un-matched like no other.

THE PHYSICAL

<u>MY LIMITATIONS</u>

Through the vernacular I express all the mystical things your able to accomplish with just a kind word from you.

My attempt to reach out and touch fall short for distance is my mortal enemy.

In a world not known to you, a false reality seems to innocently guide me, for in this place inside my mind the barriers I live with fail to exist.

Here I am comforted by all that I've yearned for, but this allusion unfair once eye's open, your not there.

MY SHOULDERS.

Her attempts to be happy
many times she's tried but
tragedy is all she knows.

Help heal her wounds and
guide her hand the trust seems
she'll never bestow- upon me
to show her care she's deserving
slowly draining the life from
me.

To gaze in her eye's look
pass her hurt, exposed her
true beauty that's her I
need.

My life on hold, set aside
all my fears, cause alone is
my existence without you.

Once her glow restored, the
pain she endured locked away,
I'll not have the strength to
continue.

DON'T LISTEN.

Loneliness has a voice all
it's own, listen closely and
it will call you.

I'd say not to answer
it's motives unclear,
could draw you in a place
unknown, in darkness
something is hiding.
        (YOUR FEARS)…

<u>WE HEAR YOU...</u>

Slowly I'm drowning in this
pool of humanity, lost I am
in complete despair.

Is any one out there
searching for me?

My signaling to the world, my
screams go unheard but refuse
(I WILL)
to wade in self-pity.

The struggle to continue an
exercise in pain, but there's
light at the end of this
journey.

For in my search, and beneath
the unknown the glow of
salvation comforts me.

<u>SLEEP TIGHT.</u>

Just beyond my reach
there exist a light, but it's
distance completely unknown.

Draw myself closer curious
to it's shine, but again my
attempts fall short.

I stand alone.

This lights brightness seems
intent on my touch but to obtain
still beyond my own sphere.

But within this glow your
silhouette has shown it holds
a power to bring me near.

Now I stand within this light,
your presence is here but still at
distance is your touch.

Should I wake from this dream
or continue to float, either way
I need you so much.

<u>GUESS WHAT.</u>

I'm in search of clarity
to deal with a loss, a feat
of my own making.

My arrogance guides me,
the price within me
refuse to share life in a
meaningful way.

To have and to hold the
words that were uttered,
what the hell was I
listening to?

<u>LIBERTY TAKEN FOR GRANTED ='S PRISON.</u>

It's there but it's elusiveness
again has dodged me.

I'm captured by it's grace for
it answers to no-one.

To posses, a treasure un-matched,
to take for granted, may despair
be your companion.

To take advantage of this, it's
secret unveiled.

Respect it or enter the gated
world of the punished.

<u>MAKING UP</u>

The years invested, time well
spent, for through it all your
love carried me.

Though time and distance
not our friend, but your
hand I ask to marry you.

In wedded bliss to live
with you, a dream that seem
far beyond our reach.

Your presence not near, great
distance separates, a lesson in
love attempted to teach.

Absences makes the heart
grow fonder the words of
a fool I'd say.

For missing this much and
being without you times I
wondered where's my lady.

Your words they cut for it's
pain I read when I looked
Upon your scribe.

If commitment this strong
and your heart can endure
Promise I'll never leave
your side.

<u>GHETTO FABULOUS</u>

The green eyed monster
of envy has entered and
left many in pain.

For jealousy the meal of
fools, corruption part of
the game.

The goal to keep up with
the jones, a fictitious
person unknown.

For to spend your time and
part of your life, in search
of a fabricated goal.

Be your own person
set the bar at your
height advice that
well should be taken.

But to chase that monster, time
a valued commodity, your life
your just straight faking…

<u>DISTANCE LOVER.</u>

You've not said a word
but within your stare I
hear everything your saying.

Your distance from me
not measurable but
your voice haunts my soul.

What we share can't be explained
to others, but to us it's
clarity and meaning comprehendible

Outside of us only one other
knows and our secret he keeps,
our expression to each other
illuminates the dark reaches
of my heart.

But allowed as you are to
explore, at peace with your touch.

I hear you and I'm answering.

Listen closely…

<u>HE'S WATCHING.</u>

The branches blow in the
whisper of the wind, God's
yawning.

The oceans churn be it
peaceful or turbulently, our
attention, he is speaking.

It's raining violently he's
crying, no longer our
attention, he's demanding.

Time to pay we're not listening…

<u>PAY</u> ATTENTION

By personal choice
solitude I choose
for to mingle is to
inter-act with fools.

My thoughts within me
guide my life, in harmony
my mind I can't lose.

This atmosphere a
danger to all, if on
guard is what your not.

For to drop your
shield find comfort
from surroundings
surely your ass has been got.

<u>UN-FINISHED</u>

Home is where the heart is,
but yet my soul seeks
shelter,
may I enter?

I DOUBT IT LITTLE SIS...

We grew together, time
taught us much but shared
we did not do.

Separated by force to find
our way alone and apart we
grew.

Blood connects us we
can't deny it's embedded
our family tree.

In time I wonder will
we learn a way to end
sibling rivalry.

UN-TITLED.

Attempts to attract not
necessary for her allure
draws many to her beauty.

The sensual curves and
exquisite lines define a
form, that to describe
merely a waste of words.

Her touch sends intense
desire to run rampant
through my blood.

To look upon her is to
Stare into the eye's of
the angelic.

Outer beauty defined as
perfection.

The quest to explore and
experience the unknown,
her inner beauty.

"TO BE CONTINUED"

<u>UNDERSTAND THE MEANING</u>

To negotiate the many obstacles
life's journey place upon you
guide the narrow straits of
the righteous and the wicked.

> To stand in judgement not our
> task, but to be judged by one
> who's supreme rule is all
> that's permitted.

Many turn a deaf ear to his
guidance for inner strength they
lack, ability to understand
ignorance and un-perceptiveness
their guide through time.

> Day of reckoning approaches,
> your concern then genuine,
> tardiness not acceptable?

AWAKEN OR SUFFER INTO
THE ABYSS...

<u>EMANCIPATE</u>

The inability to access the impure
manner in which your described
holds you firmly in place.

Intently you listen as inadequate
life forms describes your entire
race.

To form an opinion of your own,
it's danger blind they want you
to be.

The pursuit of happiness, in search
of justice, not their idea of your
liberty.

<u>GOOD MORNING</u>

Inside slumbers chambers complete
peace should be your guide.

But the journey within these halls
of the personal, the un-tapped emotion
that stir's within drives your will.

This one moment in time your world
should allow your soul to rest, the battle
rages on.

Visions of the past intrude into your future,
inner strength will find and lead you, rest on your
journey's end is near.

I TRIED.

Secretly my world slowly
crumbles around me, for what
I must express has no pleasantness
about it.

The intentions I wish to share
may do many things in terms of
your emotional well being.

My goal to respect and guard
your feelings, to introduce
sorrow a task I'm not willing
to undertake, but I must share.

I've let all that I am be your
playground, allowed as you were
to walk amongst my most guarded
treasures.

But alone you did not come,
and allowed you did let
deception be your guide and
it blinded you.

For it would not allow you to
see the depths in which your
essence was welcomed into
my soul.

But at the peak of your guides
treachery it abandoned you,
and alone you were left.

And before you all that was
given unveiled, and your
deceit replaced with shame,
for all your dreams realized.

Time healed my wounds and
strength and clarity replaced my
pain.

For this man gave in, never
to relive again.

<u>SISTAH...</u>

Within her stride mother
afrika speaks loudly, but
yet her kingdom the urban
jungles.

The light which illuminates
from her smile enough energy
to brighten any room in which
she enters.

Her words the scribe of the
egyptian queens who've
gone before her.

In her presence all men bow,
for to look upon her a beauty
un-touched by time.

Her completeness a time kept
secret, for to unlock to mere
man, surely chaos follows.

She's described as many things,
but to her inner circle she's
simply referred to as sistah.

PART OF MOTHER EARTH...

WITH HELP, I'M IN CONTROL

Placed upon me limitations
of my own making, but yet
my goals attainable.

My obstacles loom gigantic
above me but inside a will
that's carved on the face
of gilbraltar.

Advised by man to give in
to despair, to rule your
destiny, to acknowledge this
is to settle for less than
nothing.

Raise your head to the sky,
use the gifts given to you
and flourish, adversity will
bring about your best.

For it is all allah's will.

CONTROL GRANTED...

AFRIKA CALLS

Torn from the bosom of
who we knew taken to far
and distant lands.

Stripped us of our given
names replaced with a slave
owners brand.

But in us mother afrika
speaks for her voice can
never be silenced.

To treat her off-spring
much less than human, mother afrika
revenge is violence.

We choose not to stoop to a
level in which they only
understand, restore us to our
rightful spot,
back home to the mother land.

<u>WELCOME TO MY WORLD.</u>

I have been forgiven, for
in my mind I knew I was
alone and it's empty-ness
Haunted me.

Although each day I looked
into her eye's I could not
See, blinded by my own self-
Pity.

But a feeling I could not
recognize constantly
invaded my soul.

Too caught up was I to feel
what existed inside of me,
until your touch brought about
my focus.

Then the realization of
what shared my essence
became clear.

Inside me you lived, uninvited
as you were, your company
brought about my renewal.

A life un-shared truly an
Existence wasted...

<u>MY PRAYER</u>

The source of my strength lie's
beyond the stars, I feel him and
what he means to me.

A child of God who's been torn
and scarred I'm searching for my
inner peace.

Appear before me a guiding hand
so gentle to my soul.

For in his touch life's emotional
crutch will lead me and make
me whole.

I depend on him day to day
inspiration guides me through,
without his love and infinite
mercy,

I'd suffer till my life was due.

TIMES UP.

AMEN…

TOO PAINFUL

<u>CAN'T THINK ABOUT "YOU"</u>

Indecision confronts me,
thoughts of leaving intriguing
no fault of you or I.

Years not really kind to us,
for our hearts tend to wonder
but respect for what we had
still applies.

Not that I don't love anymore
complaisance just the problem
but to stay can only prolong
my pain.

But as long as I draw breath,
and thoughts do form, my
heart will bleed
every-time I hear your name.

SOUL FOOD.

It's right there in front of me,
but I can't bring myself to tell
her.

As hard as I have tried I can't
bring myself to express such coldness
although my intentions are to
respect.

But the years have shown me
her soul and all it's secrets,
but I too share a secret, one
I know will surely crush her.

Compassion a trait through her
I've acquired, which further
complicates what it is I'm
forced to do.

It's never easy, there exist no
pleasant ways to do this, but I must.

BABY YOU CAN'T COOK...

<u>LOOK AT ME...</u>

Can you hear me, for I wish not to speak above a whisper, you see the words I'll share are my hidden desires and to draw attention to myself will only lessen the effect I wish this to have.

My exterior and presence rough to it's touch, but just beneath it's surface exist compassion a fire with the ability to burn ever-lasting because of your everything.

My meaning to you I wish to keep quite simple, you see to come across wordy again just cheapens my intentions, so please as I speak look directly at me.

Your un-divided attention is necessary or you'll miss what I'm saying even if it's just my stare, you see in between my sentences, while I compose my thoughts I should still come across to you, just please look at me.

To hear me just pay attention, for what my words miss, my eye's scream to tell you.

ALL MINES...

Again I travel through thought and time, my quest to introduce a new meaning.

Displayed before me a vision,
my focus sustained because of
her intense presence

Her completeness totally envelopes
me, my yearning's call out in ways
un-describe-able and un-necessary
to attempt to explain.

Reality keeps me in check
for to drift is to become
lost in a place not familiar.

My intentions to only share
what you are, but selfishly
and only to myself.

ANTHONY L. ANDERSON

ONWARD MY LOVER….

As you walk away, I pray
you don't look back for my
memory of you is the last
word whispered from your lips.

I wish you not to turn
Around for fear you'll see me
At my weakest, and my goal
To always be your strength.

Please keep walking straight
ahead and let my smile or
touch be your guide till we
meet again.

I've begged you to not look
back, for your future is
present and my hand be
guided by you, and we
walk together into our future
memories.

NEVER IN HER PRESENCE...

What I'm dealing with now because of her, I've found the perfect cover, for manly pride refuses to let her see the effect of her words.

Just outside my window it rains profusely, but I will not stand in your presence in pain.

But she has hurt me, for she stares into my soul in search of the reward she thinks is deserving of her.

I refuse to allow her to discover why it is I stand smiling as I walk into the rain.

But just outside of her ability to comprehend this smile, the rain allows me to do what I would not let her see.

<u>INCOMPLETE.</u>

I am attempting the impossible, to place into words a description of all you mean to me.

But before I attempt this feat
allow me to apologize before I
begin, you see to sum up in words,
takes away from the impressions your
able to place on my heart.

Unfortunately it's words I must
use for your presence is lacking,
makes this task that much more
complicated.

Given the opportunity to stare into
your eye's and feel your deepness,
my exploration as to your description
broadens and to form those thoughts
in your presence my words are lost.

But again I attempt to find the
variations so please bare with me as
I search.

TO BE CONTINUED.

OBSERVATIONS.

To be heartless is not my
intention, but I feel I
must speak up for an
injustice has taken place.

You see I don't know you
but your kind and the
feelings you show are
something very familiar
to one with a soul and
the depths to feel beyond
My own.

To allow you to suffer in
silence is a crime in itself
but to know that just maybe I
hold the remedy is killing
me.

Your children are beautiful,
a reflection on what your able
to accomplish with the meager
things he's given you.

Your potential he does not
see, for his selfishness
guides him and the path it
takes only can lead you to
the arm's of another.

But because of your faith
and commitment to family
you choose to stay, and I
must be content with just
being your advisor.

But when his coldness becomes
to much to bear, there is a
warmth that exist.

Just Reach out.
Sincerely/

<u>FATHERS.</u>

Time to step up we've been delinquent
for years our turn to be real men.

We've sown our seed seen the results
but yet choose to abandon them.

A gift from God presented to you,
how precious to have and to hold,
but look at your actions your careless
gestures, how can you be that bold.

To walk away and not think twice
about the pain you've left behind,
to call yourself father you less than a
MAN,
the child will grow we can only pray,
to help redefine,

"THAT WORD"

DEFINITION IN PAIN...

All this time I walk about
with a glow of pride, for I
knew I helped create a gift
so precious that each time
my baby smiled it brought
tears to my eye's.

Who am I to be deserving of
something this overwhelming
you see clouds of darkness
were always my companion so
I never looked for my joy.

But in my child I found it,
the mother of my gift a
blessing to me, although we
weathered rough times, a
jewel we still made together,
even though times existed I
was not there, we still shared.

As my child forms into the
person he will resemble, I
see his mothers eyes and
warm smile, but a slight
un-easiness covers me for my
baby holds no likeness to me
but still yet I am a proud
father.

But in one moment my world
completely destroyed, my heart ripped
from my chest and left to rot at my
feet,
her words cut through my very
soul,
un-noticeable were her tears
only her voice I heard.

"THIS CHILD NOT YOURS"

<u>YOUR EXCUSED.</u>

At the pace in which we
started in no way we would
have thought anything could
bring about what we now face.

      What carried me through each
      day was your touch and gentle
           smile,
      but now replaced with great
      pain and heart-sick despair.

            I still love you and everytime
            your name be spoken a certain
            spark will ignite my memory of
            you, but what we've done to
            one another can't be fixed, so
            move on is our only course.

But to have known someone
so gentle a blessing not taken
for granted, your freedom you
wanted it's freely given, but take
with you the part of me that did
help you grow.

      BYE-BYE
      BABY...

6:00 A.M.

Quietly I lay here next
to you as slumber allows
your body to rest,
captivating
as they are your eye's
hidden from me.

But still I lay watching
as peace engulfs you I do
my best to lay motionless,
for I pray while you rest
it be my essence be your
dream guide.

But I've stirred you and while
I enjoyed watching your beauty as
you slept, I become lost in your
morning gaze, for I know again
it allows me the chance to relive
my night before with you.

Passion takes over, do what
you will again to reveal all
your splendor.

ANTHONY'S REASONS.

I've found comfort expressing
myself through verse, it's
allowed me the chance to
explore.

Peace of mind be my
friend for through this
passage I've located my gifts
front door.

In time I'll share all that's
come through me, but unselfishly
this task be not just my duty.

Guided by my supreme healer
I've grown in strength, never
to become weaker.

Though my words may only
comfort me, peace of mind
be my liberty.

HEARTBEAT URBAN STYLE.

Within our playground
of asphalt, steel and glass,
surrounded by the sounds
of our urban world
we find our tranquility.

Work whistles, sirens and the
screams of those who wish
to escape this madness, our
peace not entered or disturbed.

To walk amongst the many
faceless forms in tune we are
not with the distractions, but only
our heartbeats within.

Sounds we experience the daily
grinds it never changes, find your
own peace of mind...

BEAM HER UP SCOTTY...

Sat looking out my window today,
saw ya coming down the block just
as proud as you can be.

Face glowing, that certain stride
in your step as though you held the key.

Came by my window smiled at me, but
yet in your eye's I saw hunger, now in
your condition being in the motherly way
care and attention what you be needin.

But yet you walk by me heading for dat
man on the corner, you know which one,
yeah him selling a bag full of dreams.

Dat shit got you held in check, your unborn
you carry's which ya pay's your price, life
you live you gambles, roll the dice.

CRACK GOTCHA...

<u>BABY TAKE HIM OFF FOR A WHILE."</u>

My world's cold, I don't feel
nothing but a place for me I
must carve.

Empty shell of existence, slave to
the 9 to 5 man's got a brother
living real hard.

Come home to my baby weight of
the world got me, I can't seem to
shake this monkey.

That certain smile she gives, her tender
love and care, monkey placed on the shelf,
must take time to show her she is
relevant.

A.I.D.S.

I'm proud of you son,
for you've come through so much
adversity in this world.

The thug's, drug runners and dealers
you've avoided and kept your focus,
your many dreams we've spoken about.

Life's not been an easy thing for our
family, but look into your mothers
eye's and see her pride and joy in you.

But where are you going my child, why
through all this adversity do I still see
pain in you.

Has this world made you cold and unfeeling,
or is this just a phase of adolescents.

I love you son, proud of you too,
damn shame though, fought off the ghetto
world for as long as you did, but look
what's taken you.

<u>SHE'S ON THE MOVE.</u>

My child's going to do many things,
the many dreams I want her to reach, why would this
cruel world show her pain in each lesson it
wishes to teach.

In front of my baby the world unfolds
she searches for what will make her happy
complete and whole.

Obstacles not a problem, with the grace of
a gazelle she leaps over and around them.

Although her young life just begins,
only thing can slow her down (NOT STOP HER),
that's hate and racism.

STRIVE YOUNG SISTAH.

NO MORE LOVE FOR US...

Excuse me but it's time we
talk wouldn't you think,
that has gone on long enough
and what's come out of it.

Nothing either one of us can
use, but something we can both
do without, once upon a time
I saw your glow.

But it would appear now when I
enter a room disgust has replaced
affection and that's hurtful.

For even though my feelings have
altered I still, when I look deep,
see my dreams shattered, but still
a life time of respect will stay,
your importance will always be a
priority to me.

This can't be salvaged, too much
damage has already been done,
but once anger has left and we
both calm down, please don't
keep me from my son.

Never did I mean to hurt you
stupidity held my hand, but
my flesh and blood that child
is to me.

And my responsibility's to him.
He must know not only his
father, but a man.

THE HARDEST WORD...

Although time has covered the serious wound that's been placed upon your heart, the words I know that need to be said are lost deep within my thoughts.

In my life I've done my wrongs and punished I now stand and take, but please allow me if you will, help me bury their existing hate.

To turn back the clock and start anew, a dream that's seen in my mind, help me find peace and the proper words, and heal their wounds at their pace, and somewhere in their own time.

There's only one thing that I can say but it fixes absolutely nothing, but till I'm placed in a box, I'll be forever

SORRY...

ANTHONY L. ANDERSON

<u>GUESS YOU WASN'T...</u>

My style was not to make you
feel guilty, but I know what
you've done.

I could have gotten angry and
made you feel like a child, but
also not my way, slowly I move on.

To rant and rave for what has happened
could have been allowed,
but to who's gain.

My feelings I choose to guard,
and grant you the mis-fortune of
being a fool.

YOU WERE NOT KISSING ONE.

BLACK TRULY IS BEAUTIFUL

Completely blinded she was,
for she see's not her exquisiteness
nor does her chocolate complexion
give her the confidence it rightfully
deserves.

If only she were allowed to observe
her nakedness through the eye's of
another, she would know the beauty
her reflection cast amongst the sky.

<u>LUST x 2 = AGAIN...</u>

In the name of love our hearts
we gave till sleep peacefully captured us.

The night of passion thinking only of
pleasure, but blindly we were led by
pure lust.

But alive I am to love again a blessing
in itself, my heart be yours, my body still
trembles, knowing again your touch soon
be felt...

WHAT ABOUT IT.

We shall over-come,
over-come we shall
somebody should have
taught your ass to duck.

Promise land we still
search for- search for we
still look, promise you
this what you search for
good luck.

Lunch counters we attempt
to sit at, while dat man
constantly spit at, you really
need to eat at that man's place.

Corporate world you want in,
american dream to fit in, while
oppressors slowly kills off the
afrikan race.

DON'T RESPOND...

In many circles I'm someone who can
carry a conversation about anything of
importance.

I even dare say I can relate to some
of the brightest minds and be able to
impress.

A genius I definitely am not, but I do
my best to comprehend all that surrounds
me.

But for all my knowledge, why is it when
you with that seductive walk, you with
the smile to light the darkest night,

Yes I'm speaking about you with a touch
so hot would make hells fire seem like a
spark.

Be able to silence not only my words,
But also my heart-beat?

<u>MONEY GET YOU NOTHING...</u>

You could say I've been blessed with privilege,
for I have been able to run and play with
the jet set.

It would be fair to say I could see the world
a hundred or more times and cost be no object.

With all that's been afforded to me for years to
come live lavishly and exist in a world many only
dream about and never see.

I do pretend I have everything and my life is one
so very sweet.

But without your gentle touch, and warm smile, my
life truly feels incomplete.

YOU'VE ALL THE ANSWERS...

Something's very wrong isn't it?

You see within your touch I was lost and alone.

You were not there, where are you?

As we laid there into your eye's I look and felt your absence.

Why does distance separate us?

Every word I spoke to hear you reply felt as if a stranger laid next to me.

I understand nothing you said.

Is there something you need to tell me?

Are you coming back?

Do you wish for me to continue to live in the darkness?

In the light is where our bond to each started, are you now committing me back to that world?

Settle my mind, don't leave it like this, when did you grow so cold and away from me.

Your feelings I've always protected do I really deserve to be crushed?

DID I DESERVE THIS?

<u>VOICES FROM INSIDE.</u>

It's hard to write a poem in prison,
to think beyond these walls, to expose
your thoughts to those around you
guard your manhood at all cost.

But my voice I must let sound and
refuse to give in, for within these bars
of pain and strife till I'm dead.

Forge on till I win.

Can't let despair rule my world I still
have much to give, a life shut down to
be silenced by this place.

I'll find a way to live.

The words I've placed to paper can be
related to.

Locked away from the world our
voices cry out to you.

ABOUT THE AUTHOR

Born in the south and raised in the cities of the north, this first time author attempts to relate his life experiences to those who can feel and live the frustrations, anger, and the emotional ride that make up life. To place such personal feelings in this form tends to give personal therapy to this writer, but his goals are to touch the brothers and sisters who handle the day to day struggle and survival of the hood.